Heroes for Young Readers

Written by Renee Taft Meloche
Illustrated by Bryan Pollard

Adoniram Judson	Gladys Aylward
Amy Carmichael	Hudson Taylor
Betty Greene	Ida Scudder
Brother Andrew	Jim Elliot
Cameron Townsend	Jonathan Goforth
Corrie ten Boom	Loren Cunningham
C. S. Lewis	Lottie Moon
David Livingstone	Mary Slessor
Eric Liddell	Nate Saint
George Müller	William Carey

Heroes of History for Young Readers

Written by Renee Taft Meloche
Illustrated by Bryan Pollard

Daniel Boone
Clara Barton
George Washington
George Washington Carver
Meriwether Lewis

...and more coming soon

*Heroes for Young Readers Activity Guides and audio CDs
are now available! See the back of this book for more information.*

For a free catalog of books and materials contact
YWAM Publishing, P.O. Box 55787, Seattle, WA 98155
1-800-922-2143 www.ywampublishing.com

HEROES FOR YOUNG READERS

ERIC LIDDELL

Running for a Higher Prize

Written by Renee Taft Meloche
Illustrated by Bryan Pollard

YWAM
PUBLISHING
P.O. BOX 55787   SEATTLE, WA 98155

Eric Liddell: Running for a Higher Prize   Text © 2001 by Renee Taft Meloche   Illustrations © 2001 by Bryan Pollard
Published by YWAM Publishing, P.O. Box 55787, Seattle, WA 98155   ISBN 978-1-57658-230-5   Printed in China.   All rights reserved.

A Scottish boy named Eric Liddell
        thought the greatest fun
was moving fast just like the wind:
        he simply loved to run.

He loved to sprint so very much
        that he began to dream
of one day running on Great Britain's
        fine Olympic team.

As he grew up, he soon became
        impossible to beat,
for he excelled in every sport;
        he had the fastest feet.

When playing rugby or when racing
        Eric was the star.
No other boys could catch him since
        he was the best by far.

He knew that he was blessed by God
        at birth with special speed.
He planned to use this gift to help
        inspire and to lead.

So when Olympic trials were held
    in London, in July,
in nineteen hundred twenty-three,
    he went; he had to try.

He'd trained to win two races, first
    the hundred-meter run.
He shook the other racers' hands
    before the starting gun.

He took a trowel and dug two holes
    to get a better start,
then loaned it out, for he played fair
    and had a generous heart.

He crouched down at the starting line.
Exhaled. Tucked his chin.
He focused toward the finish line.
He set his mind to win.

The gun went off. The race began.
It ended just as fast.
That day he set a record in
the hundred-meter dash.

His next race was a harder one—
    two-twenty-meters long,
and though this took more stamina
    he won it looking strong.

So Eric was Great Britain's brightest
    hope to win first place
the next year at the great world games;
    he hadn't lost a race.

When Eric raced the next week, though,
       a runner tried to pass,
and accidentally tripped him, knocking
       Eric to the grass.

Though Eric now was twenty yards
       behind the running pack,
he sprang up to his feet and pumped
       his legs, his head thrown back,
and with a super burst of speed
       he ran his very best
and dashed across the finish line
       ahead of all the rest!

While Eric loved to run so much,
    there's something he loved more.
For Eric was a Christian man
    and that's what he lived for.

When people came to hear him talk
    of how he loved to run,
he also took the chance to speak
    about God and His Son.

He never took full credit for
    awards that he had won,
but gratefully thanked God from whom
    all blessings really come.

Just months before the games were held
         he suddenly withdrew,
because his races were on Sunday—
         that he would not do.

For Sunday was a day for God—
         to honor Him and rest.
He simply would not run that day,
         although he was the best.

As papers spread the news that Eric
         would no longer run,
all Britain was unhappy, for
         they knew he would have won.

And just because he made this choice—
         in many people's eyes—
he was a traitor. Eric, though,
         refused to compromise.

The heads of Britain's team found his
       decision a disgrace,
but asked if he'd compete in the
       four-hundred-meter race,
a race not held on Sunday. This
       at first seemed like good news.
But Eric hadn't trained to run
       that far—and he could lose.

Still Eric said, "I'll do it!" In
       July of twenty-four
he sailed across the English Channel
       onto France's shore.

And at the opening ceremony
      Eric felt so proud
to walk in with the British team
      and see the stadium crowd.

The Union Jack unfurled and the
      Olympic flag flew high.
White pigeons were let go and
      thousands flew up to the sky.

The cannons boomed, and sixty thousand
      fans rose up and cheered.
The whole crowd was expectant. Then
      a British lord appeared.

He shook each athlete's hand but Eric's—
      stared at him instead.
"To play the game is all that matters
      in one's life," he said.

It was quite clear to Eric what
      the man was trying to say:
he may have had a chance for gold
      and thrown it all away.

But even if he'd heard those words
      from Britain's only king,
he knew a game in life was not
      the most important thing.

To honor God was so much greater
      than vast wealth or fame,
or winning a gold medal at
      the grand Olympic Games.

Now Eric knew the other runners
     would be hard to beat.
Their times were faster than his own
     when each one ran his heat.

Of six men in the finals, Eric
     was the shortest one.
To run four hundred took long legs.
     Would Eric be outrun?

He heard the sound of bagpipes and
was quite surprised to see
some Scottish pipers march in step
while playing right on key
an old familiar Scottish tune
to cheer their Scotsman on.
So Eric waved and smiled at them
and softly hummed along.

He reached into his pocket and
he found inside a note
on which a teammate had put down
a favorite Bible quote:
"Whoever honors me," it said,
"I too will honor him."
Then Eric knew his choice was right
regardless of who'd win.

The bagpipe music faded and
    with growing, deep suspense,
the runners took their places: they
    were feeling tight and tense.

Get ready. Set. A shot rang out.
    There was no looking back.
The runners' feet beat fast and hard
    against the cinder track.

As Eric ran around the bend,
      he thought that he would see
some runners out in front of him
      but found, surprisingly,
that he was in first place. As beads
      of sweat formed on his brow,
he willed his body to go faster.
      Faster. Faster now!

He crossed the finish line in less
          than fifty seconds flat;
collapsed into his coach's arms,
          exhausted. Then he sat
and heard loud cheers and clapping from
          the crowd who'd gathered there.
His British coach was beaming and
          soon Eric was aware
that he had won and set a new
          Olympic record too.
Against all odds he had defeated
          all the runners who
had once seemed so unbeatable.
          Now Eric felt the thrill
of living his Olympic dream—
          it seemed a miracle.

While Scotland hailed young Eric as
        its new heroic star,
he chose to leave his land behind
        and go to live afar
in China, where he taught the Chinese
        college students there—
English, rugby, chemistry—
        and when they grew aware
that Eric Liddell had won gold
        at the Olympic Games,
they all were puzzled by this news.
        They wondered why he came
when he had so much honor in
        his country back at home
and why he'd left it all behind
        for this land, not his own.

So during Bible study, Eric
        took the time to share
that all the fame and honor he'd
        received could not compare
to serving others with his life
        and honoring his Lord,
for God and His great love and truth
        are what we should run toward.

Now Eric did not live as long
        as many people do.
When he was forty-three years old
        his life on earth was through.

He'd always liked the short race, not
        a long, long marathon,
and similarly Eric's life
        did not go on and on.

And now he lives with God since he
        has finished this life's race,
and when he was a champion here
        he put God in first place.

Christian Heroes: Then & Now

by Janet and Geoff Benge

Heroes for Young Readers and Heroes of History for Young Readers are based on the Christian Heroes: Then & Now and Heroes of History biographies by Janet and Geoff Benge. Don't miss out on these exciting, true adventures for ages ten and up!

Continued on the next page...

Heroes of History

by Janet and Geoff Benge

Abraham Lincoln: A New Birth of Freedom
Alan Shepard: Higher and Faster
Benjamin Franklin: Live Wire
Christopher Columbus: Across the Ocean Sea
Clara Barton: Courage under Fire
Daniel Boone: Frontiersman
Douglas MacArthur: What Greater Honor
George Washington Carver: From Slave to Scientist
George Washington: True Patriot
Harriet Tubman: Freedombound
John Adams: Independence Forever
John Smith: A Foothold in the New World
Laura Ingalls Wilder: A Storybook Life
Meriwether Lewis: Off the Edge of the Map
Orville Wright: The Flyer
Theodore Roosevelt: An American Original
Thomas Edison: Inspiration and Hard Work
William Penn: Liberty and Justice for All

...and more coming soon. Unit Study Curriculum Guides are also available.

Heroes for Young Readers Activity Guides
Educational and Character-Building Lessons for Children

by Renee Taft Meloche

Heroes for Young Readers Activity Guide for Books 1–4
Gladys Aylward, Eric Liddell, Nate Saint, George Müller

Heroes for Young Readers Activity Guide for Books 5–8
Amy Carmichael, Corrie ten Boom, Mary Slessor, William Carey

Heroes for Young Readers Activity Guide for Books 9–12
Betty Greene, David Livingstone, Adoniram Judson, Hudson Taylor

Heroes for Young Readers Activity Guide for Books 13–16
Jim Elliot, Cameron Townsend, Jonathan Goforth, Lottie Moon
Heroes of History for Young Readers Activity Guide for Books 1–4
George Washington Carver, Meriwether Lewis, George Washington, Clara Barton

...and more coming soon.

Designed to accompany the vibrant Heroes for Young Readers books, these fun-filled Activity Guides lead young children through a variety of character-building and educational activities. Pick and choose from the activities or follow the included thirteen-week syllabus. An audio CD with book readings, songs, and fun activity tracks is available for each Activity Guide.

For a free catalog of books and materials contact
YWAM Publishing, P.O. Box 55787, Seattle, WA 98155
1-800-922-2143 www.ywampublishing.com